POEMS

Gabriela Dulce

POEMS

Gabriela Dulce

First Printing: December 2018

ISBN 978-0-9991187-3-3 paperback

Contact: portreecer@yahoo.com

Available for order online

Table of Contents

Dandelion

It's full of wishes
It's fierce and has a roar
People call it a weed
But I know it's the queen

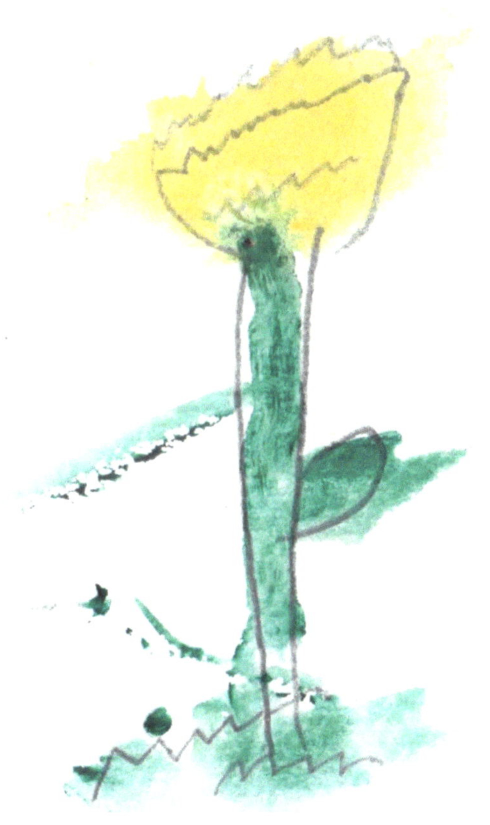

Run

A girl runs
You can tell by her face she's not having fun
Her hair drawn up in a bun
Where is she running
When will she stop
Her mind thinking of what people have done
No one is chasing her but yet she runs
Run
Run
Run
She runs to a hill with a grave
She gets down on her knees and cries

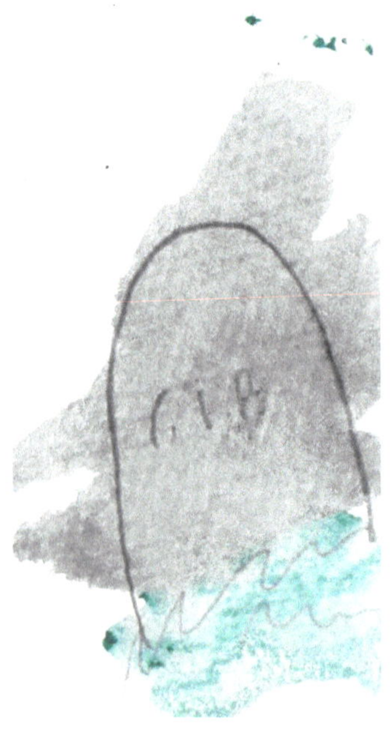

Silly boy

Silly boy you called me weird
But you really should know
Weird's just another word for extraordinaire

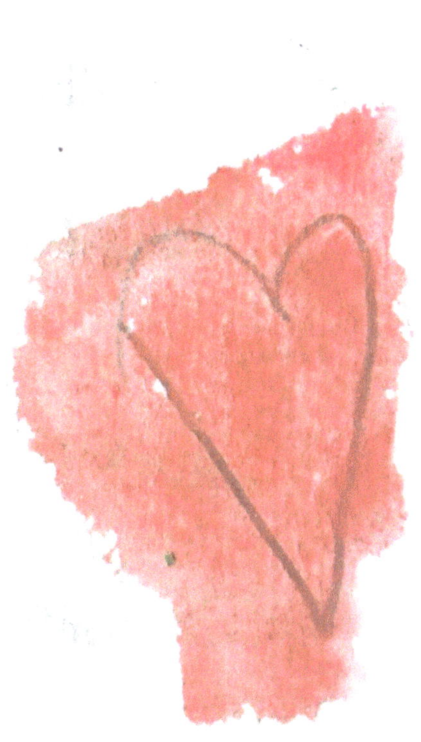

Love can overcome

Love can overcome all
Love can overcome fear
Love can overcome pain
Love can overcome all

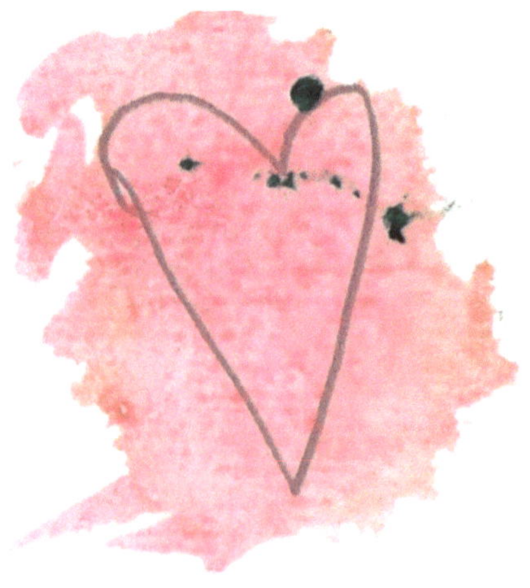

I could

I could be a goddess
But I'd rather be modess
I could be mean
But I'd rather be green
I could ditch my friends and go to France
But I'd rather take a chance
I could litter
But I'd rather help make our planet fitter
I could do a thousand or a million things
But for every choice I made and every chance I take
I'd rather choose right than wrong and good over bad

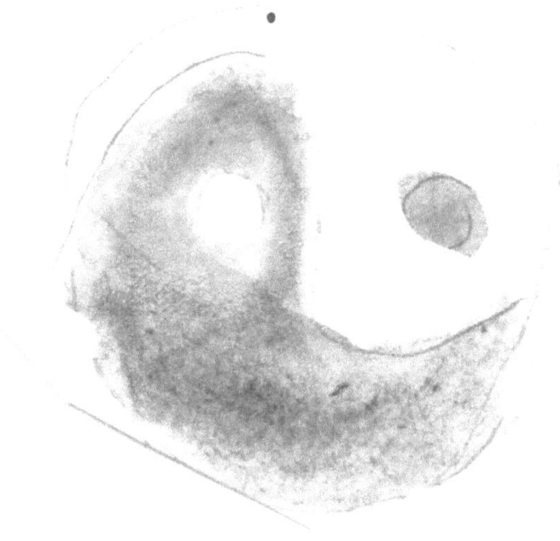

My Heart is a Wall

My Heart is a wall that will never fall
If a flood of temptation tries to break it down it will stand tall
If a tsunami of fear tries to cover it it will rise up
If an army of lies tries to tear it down it will fight them off
Though nations and leaves may fall my heart will never

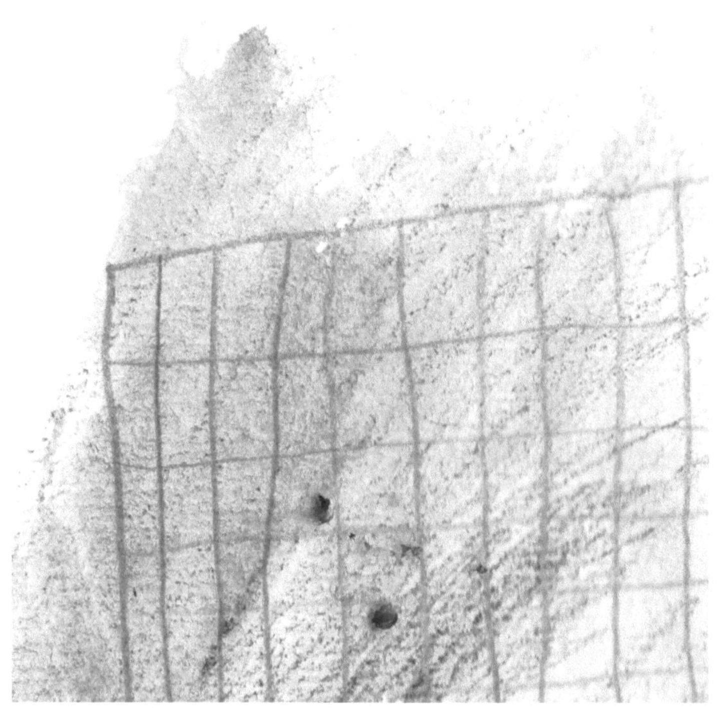

Rainbow

After the rain when the sun comes out
A rainbow forms in the sky
I wonder how I wonder why
A gift from the sky

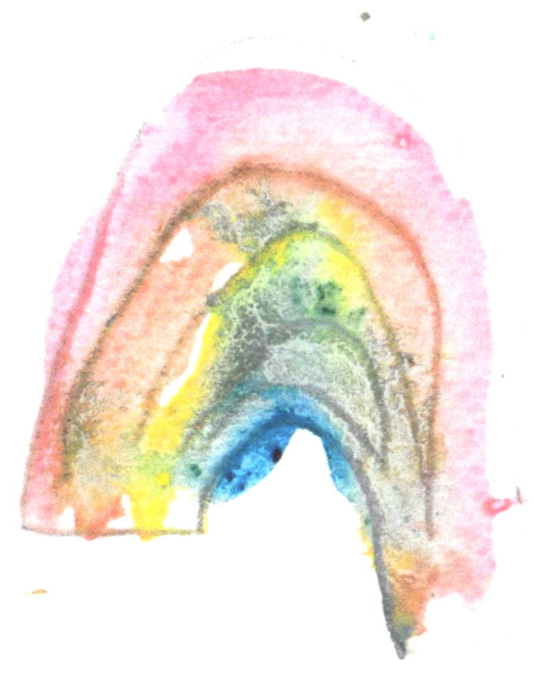

The wind

Run with the wind
Climb with the wind
Live with the wind.

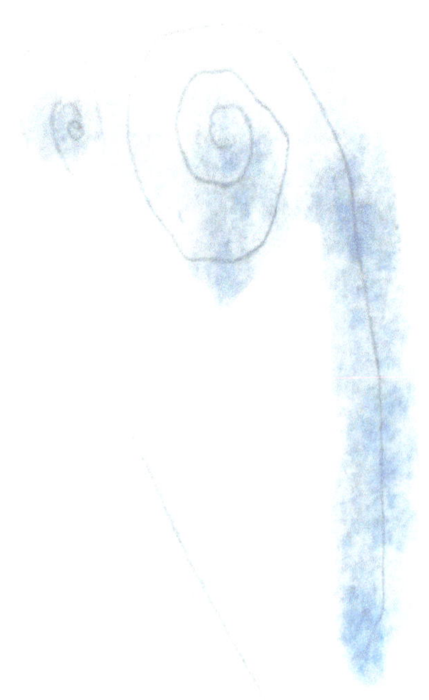

Whoosh

a girl went in the woods
"Whoosh whoosh" went the wind
"Creek creek" goes the trees
"Help help" screams the girl

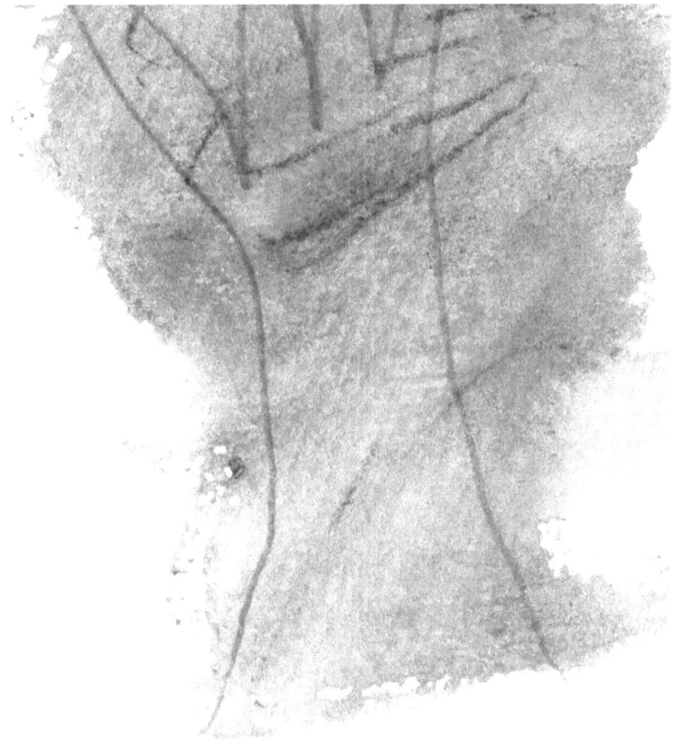

Fly

Fly little birdie go
Reach for the stars
Fly all night
Fly little birdie go
Don't be scared to go go go

Balloon

I let go
I cried a little
But who knows maybe I'll see it again soon
I miss you balloon

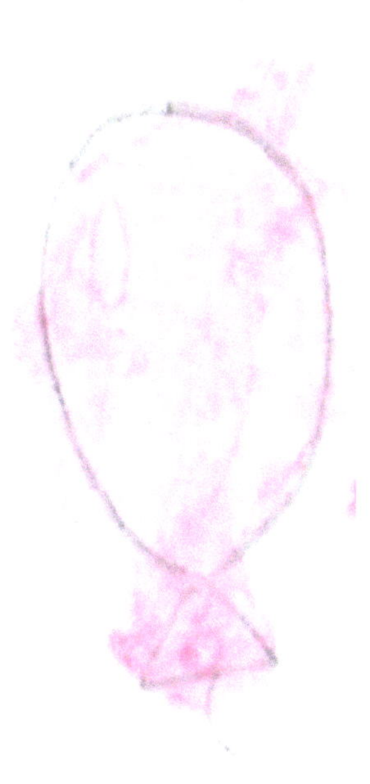

Clouds

There fluffy
Big and small
Thousands of shapes

Rain

Most people want the rain to stop
But I want it to go on
The flowers are watered
Rainbows are made
So rain please stay

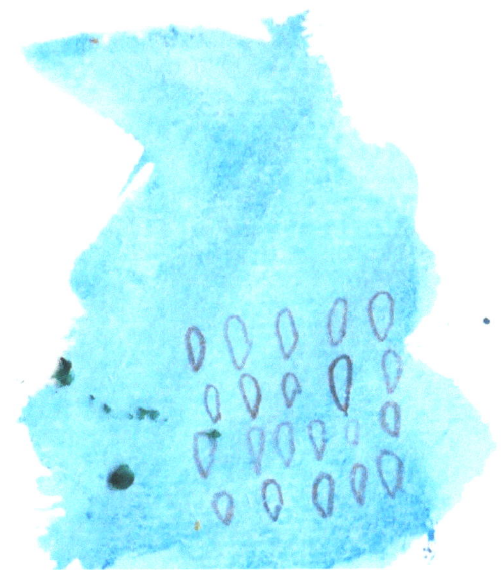

The sea

The rocking of the waves
The birds squawking
I know this is my home

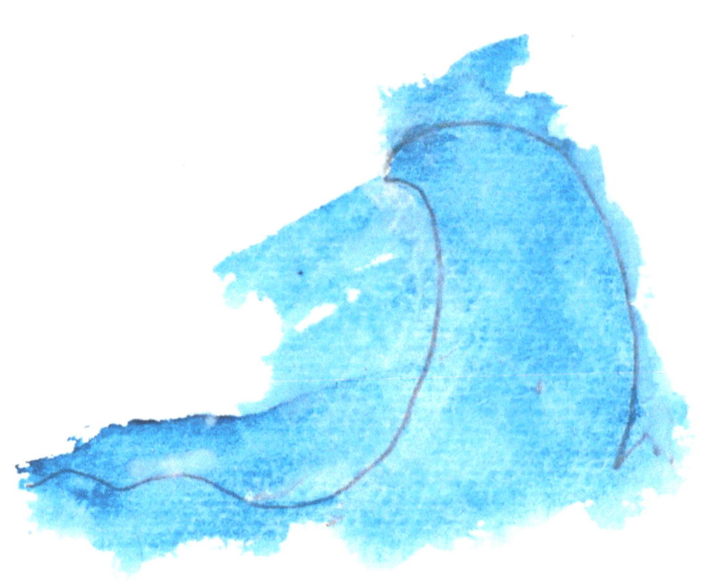

New year

It's the new year
The sky is blue
The cheer is here
It's the new year

Stars

The stars shine bright
A diamond of light
Up in the sky
Stars shine a hope

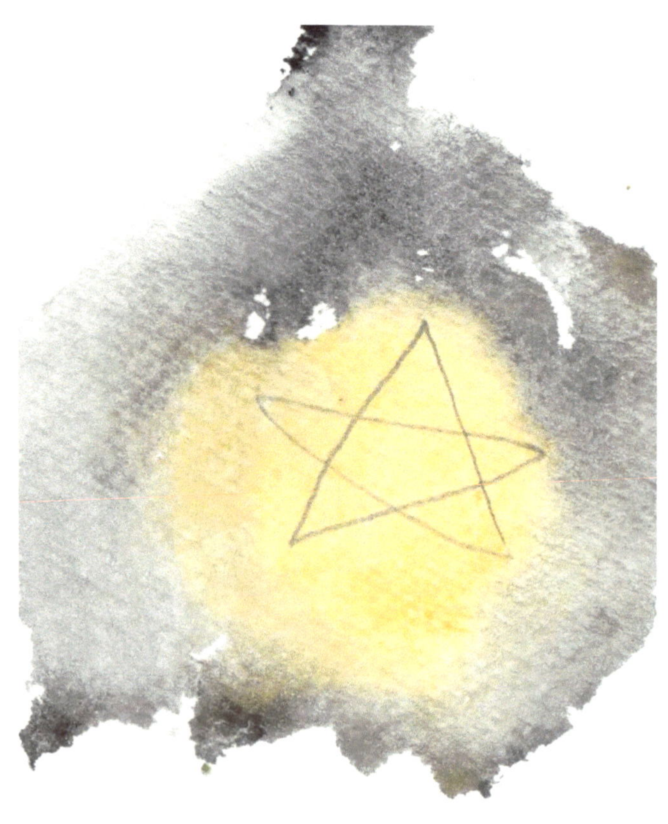

Moonlight

Where the moon shines on the beach making the water glow
that's where you'll find me
In the clearing in the forest where the moon shines bright
that's where you'll find me
Let the moonlight guide you to me

Sun

Oh how I love fun in the sun
I can run
I can climb
Oh how I love fun in the sun

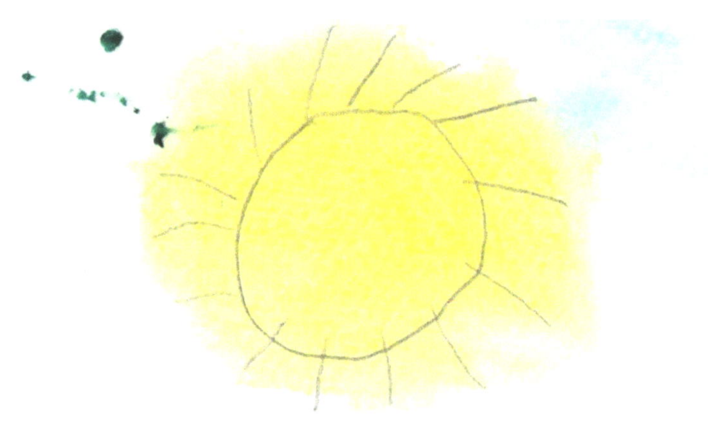

Breakfast

Pancakes with syrup
Butter with rolls
Eggs with toast
It is a break feast

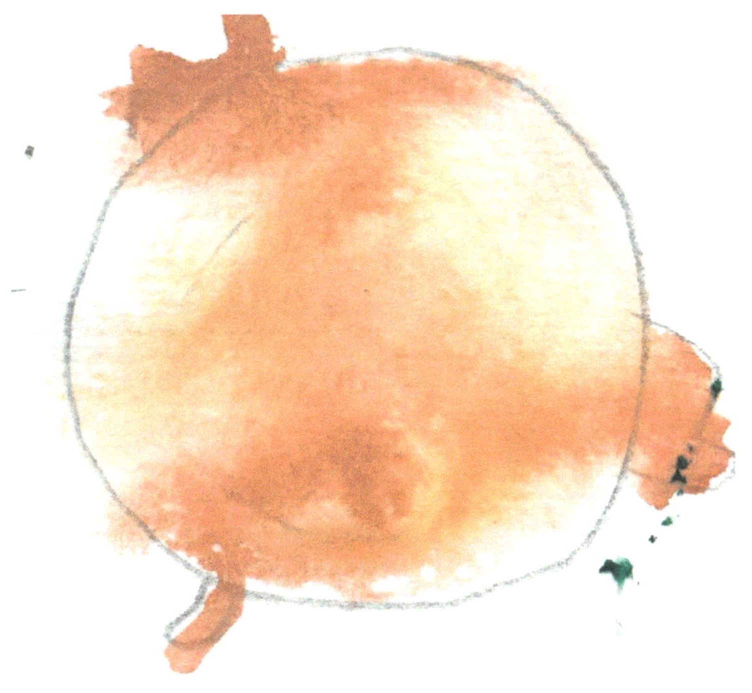

What I saw

I was walking on the street and heard faint music
I saw a window with the lights on
Inside a man and a woman were dancing
Then the man dipped the woman and they kissed

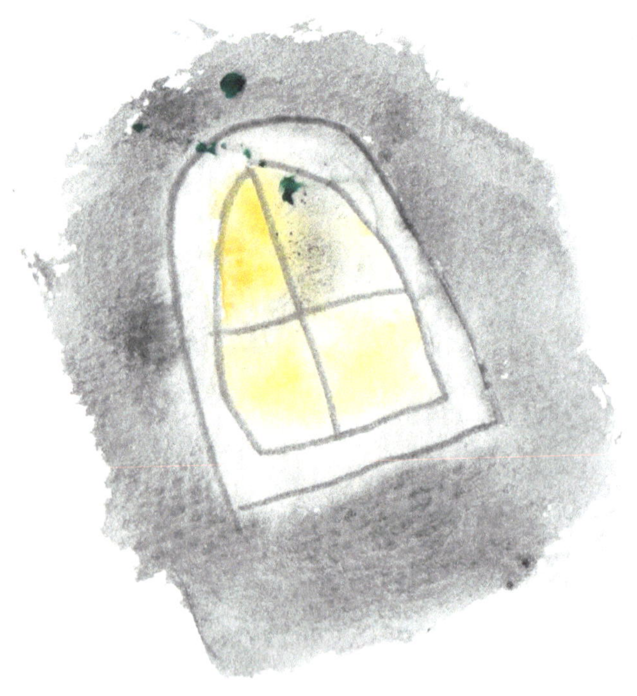

Treetop

I climbed up this tree
My mom tells me to get down
But I can't come down
Up here it's just me
Down there it's everything
Though it's extremely hot
And to anyone that sees me it looks like I'm in an uncomfortable spot
But up here I'm finally on top

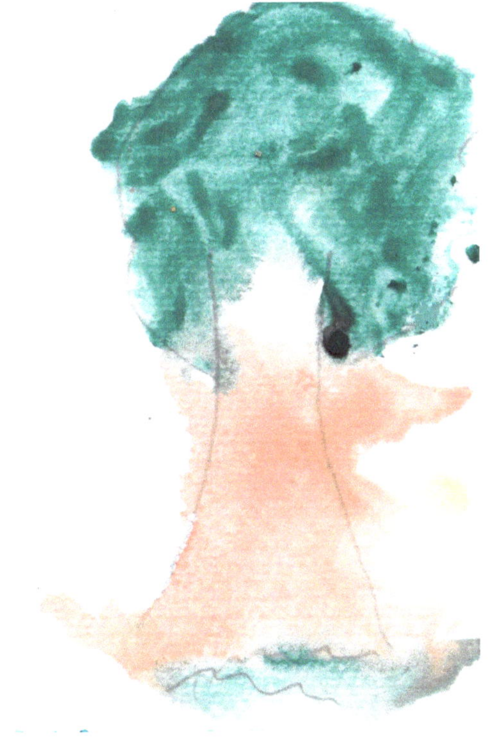

The little chipmunk

The little chipmunk ran through the woods
The little chipmunk ran to a path
The little chipmunk ran into my backyard

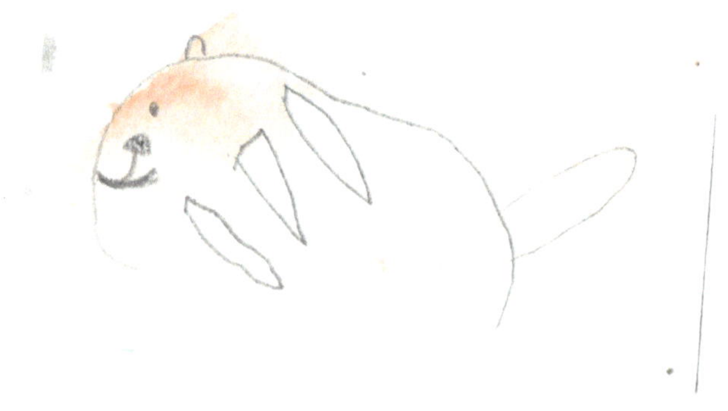

Hi

Hi
Hello
I hate to say goodbye but I must go

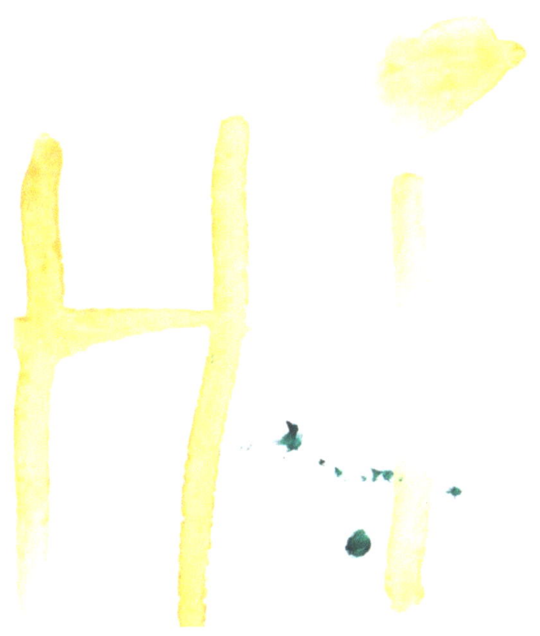

Reach

Happiness is in reach, dreams are in reach, kindness is in reach
Kindness is in reach, kindness is in reach so stop making people cry
Dreams are in reach, so stop throwing them away
Happiness is in reach and it's about your attitude so start trying to be positive
There is a reason our world is growing problems and it's our fault for never reaching
but maybe just maybe if we start reaching most of the problems will end

www.ingramcontent.com/pod-product-compliance
Lightning Source LLC
LaVergne TN
LVHW052311100826
845147LV00006B/727